Around the World in a Single Day

Happy House

About Wise & Wide

- A systematic 6-level English reading program based on Lexile® measures
- Diverse and interesting topics chosen from the elementary curriculums of Korea and English speaking western countries
- Well-written books in various forms including fiction stories, descriptive texts, and classics retold
- The informative but original fiction stories grab your interest, leading to the easy and clear understanding of the educational content.
- Improve thinking skills with solid after-reading activities at all levels of the series.

Wise & Wide is a 6-level English reading program that consists of 60 books and each level is systematically divided by Lexile® measures. The Lexile® Framework for Reading is the most popular reading measuring system in American formal education curriculums and many English programs. Over 20 out of 50 states in the U.S. mark Lexile® measures directly on students' final report cards and over 300 well-known publishers adopt and use Lexile® measures.

Experience many kinds of readings written by professional writers from the U.S. and England. They used interesting topics that were carefully chosen after analyzing elementary curriculums from around the world including Korea, the U.S., England, and Australia among many others. Comprehensive after-reading activities including graphic organizers, speaking tasks, and After-reading Tests are ready for you.

Levels in the series and their corresponding Lexile® measures

Level	Lexile® measures	U.S. Grade
Level 1	Below 200L	Pre K - K
Level 2	190L - 400L	Lower Grade 1
Level 3	350L - 530L	Upper Grade 1
Level 4	420L - 650L	Grade 2
Level 5	520L - 940L	Grade 3 - 4
Level 6	830L - 1070L	Grade 5 - 6

* Smart Readers: Wise & Wide level 1 is applicable to the preschool level in the U.S.
* The source of the relationship between Lexile® measures and U.S. school grades: CCSS(Common Core State Standards) FOR ENGLISH LANGUAGE ARTS, APPENDIX A (2012, which is used by 45 states in the U.S.)

Topic List

	Level 1	Level 2	Level 3	Level 4	Level 5	Level 6
Book 1	Science〉Biology: The hibernation of animals Story	Science〉Biology: Living and nonliving things Story	Science〉Biology〉 Animals & the Environment: Sea otters Story	Environment〉 Living with nature: The diver & the persimmon tree Story	Science〉Biology: Animal: Amazing animals of the Amazon Story	Science〉Biology: Germs, transmitted diseases Story
Book 2	Literature〉 World classics: Aesop's fables Story	Literature〉 Traditional fairy tale: Old tales about stones Story	Social Studies〉 Economy: To run a business to make and save money Story	Science〉Biology〉 Plants: Photosynthesis Story	Science〉Earth science: Earth's layers, earthquakes, volcanoes, and earth's atmosphere Report	Mathematics〉 Sequence: The golden ratio & the Fibonacci sequence Story
Book 3	Science〉Physics: How shadows are formed Story	Literature〉 World classics: Peter Pan Story	Science〉Scientific technology: Nanobots Story	Literature〉Myths: World's creation stories Story	Literature〉 Legend: The story of King Arthur Story	Literature〉Myths: Constellation myths Story
Book 4	Literature〉 Traditional literature: The Talmud Story	Science〉Biology〉 Animal: Polar bears Story	Science〉Biology〉 Animal: Mountain gorillas Story	Social Studies〉 Cultural anthropology: Amazing ancient cultures of the world Story	Science〉 Earth science: Clouds and weather Story	Literature〉 Human & animals: The friendship between a girl and a horse Story
Book 5	Social Studies〉 Ethics: Rules in daily life Story	Science〉Biology〉 The five senses Report	Social Studies〉 Cultural anthropology: Astonishing festivals Report	Art〉Music: Stories from two operas Story	Social Studies〉 World culture & history: The Renaissance Story	Sports〉 Board sports: Surfing & snowboarding Story
Book 6	Social Studies〉 World geography & travel: Tourist attractions around the world Story	Science〉Biology〉 Animal: Dinosaurs Story	Science〉 Astronomy: The solar system Story	Social Studies〉 People: Three great people who overcame hardships Story	Science〉Scientific technology: The wonderful world of robots Report	Art〉Music: Composers of the Romantic Era Report
Book 7	Science〉 Space science: The life of astronauts Report	Social Studies〉 Cultural anthropology: Mythological monsters from around the world Report	Mathematics〉 Elementary mathematics: Numbers, measurement, shapes and data Report	Science & Social Studies〉 Technology & culture: Inventions from around the world Report	Art〉Works of art: Famous paintings Report	Social Studies〉 Human & animals: Animals in action for human Report
Book 8	Social Studies〉 Cultural anthropology: Various living cultures of the world Story	Art〉Music: Instruments in the orchestra Story	Social Studies〉 Life safety: Learning and using outdoor survival skills Story	Social Studies〉 History: The California Gold Rush Report	Social Studies & Science〉 Psychology: Psychology in everyday life Story	Literature〉 World classics: The Merchant of Venice Story
Book 9	Social Studies〉 Jobs: Interviews about jobs Report	Science〉Scientific technology: Developments in technology in different times Story	Social Studies〉 Politics〉Election: Running for 3rd grade class president Story	Literature〉 World classics: Stories of Sherlock Holmes Story	Literature〉 World classics: Adrift in the Pacific Story	
Book 10		Sports〉Winter sports: Various aspects of some Winter Olympic sports Report				

* 10 books in each level will be published.

How to Use
This Book

•Before Reading

You can easily find the topic and what kind of story you are about to read.

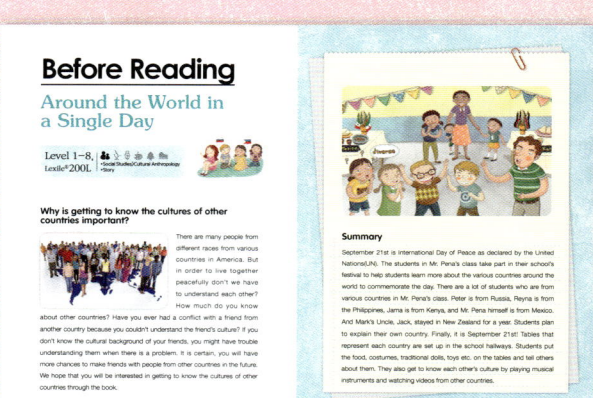

•The text

All the stories were written by professional writers from the U.S. and England, so you will read authentic and appropriate English sentences and expressions in every book in the series.

•Pop Quiz

Check out right away if you understand what you have just read by solving a pop quiz that checks your comprehension.

•Key Words

The key words and expressions on each page are listed for you to easily study them.

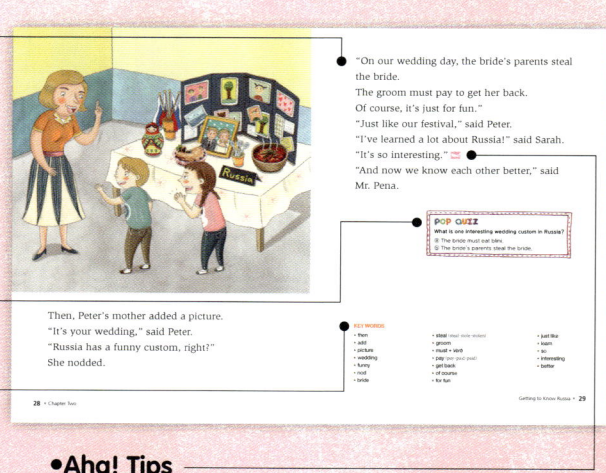

•Aha! Tips

Download free Korean explanations at *www.ihappyhouse.co.kr* for all of the sentences marked with "Aha!". These explain cultural scientific, and economic knowledge or they deal with aspects of English such as grammatical structures or idiomatic expressions. There are lots of "Aha! Tips" to help you understand the text.

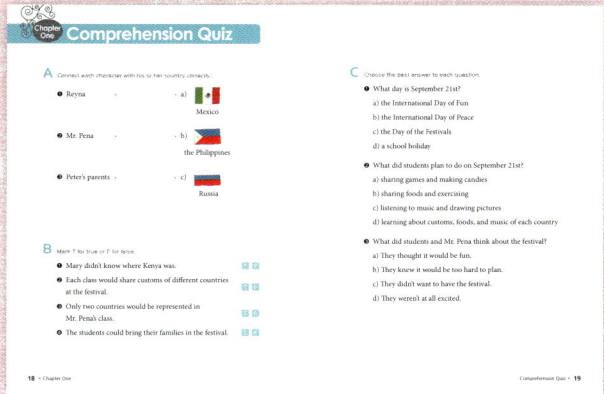

•Comprehension Quiz

After reading one chapter, solve various questions to find out if you fully understand the content.

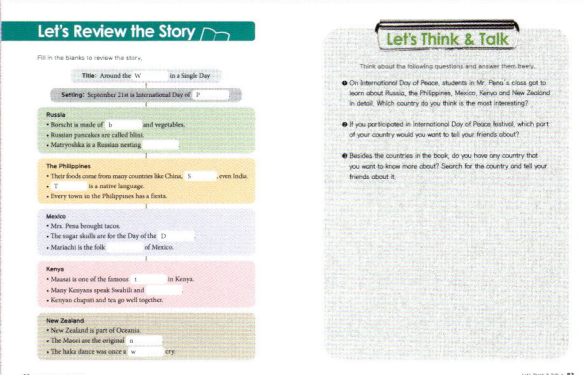

•Let's Review the Story /
•Let's Think & Talk

Fill in the blanks in the organizer to summarize the whole story. Express your own thinking and feelings about the story by answering the questions. You can build up logic and reasoning skills for your essay examinations in the future.

Appendix

Audio CD

In the CD audio book form, the texts are read vividly by American professional voice actors. (MP3 files downloaded for free)

After-reading Test

Solve an additionally provided After-reading Test for each book.

The Korean translation, Answer Keys, a Word Quiz, a Word List, and Aha! Tips for each book

You can download them for free at *www.ihappyhouse.co.kr* or *www.darakwon.co.kr*

Before Reading

Around the World in a Single Day

Level 1−8,
Lexile® 200L

•Social Studies)Cultural Anthropology
•Story

Why is getting to know the cultures of other countries important?

There are many people from different races from various countries in America. But in order to live together peacefully don't we have to understand each other? How much do you know about other countries? Have you ever had a conflict with a friend from another country because you couldn't understand the friend's culture? If you don't know the cultural background of your friends, you might have trouble understanding them when there is a problem. It is certain, you will have more chances to make friends with people from other countries in the future. We hope that you will be interested in getting to know the cultures of other countries through the book.

Summary

September 21st is International Day of Peace as declared by the United Nations(UN). The students in Mr. Pena's class take part in their school's festival to help students learn more about the various countries around the world to commemorate the day. There are a lot of students who are from various countries in Mr. Pena's class. Peter is from Russia, Reyna is from the Philippines, Jama is from Kenya, and Mr. Pena himself is from Mexico. And Mark's Uncle, Jack, stayed in New Zealand for a year. Students plan to explain their own country. Finally, it is September 21st! Tables that represent each country are set up in the school hallways. Students put the food, costumes, traditional dolls, toys etc. on the tables and tell others about them. They also get to know each other's culture by playing musical instruments and watching videos from other countries.

Contents

Around the World in a Single Day

Around the World
in a Single Day

Mr. Pena stood in front of the class.

"I have big news," he said.

The first graders were excited.

They didn't want to miss a word!

"September 21st is International Day of Peace.

Our school will celebrate!"

Anne raised her hand.

"Will we have a party?"

"Yes, a festival," said Mr. Pena.

"We have students from around the world.

Each class will share about countries.

It's a way for us to build peace."

KEY WORDS

- big
- news
- stand (stand-stood-stood)
- in front of
- class
- first
- grader
- excited
- want
- miss
- word
- September
- International Day of Peace (*cf.* international)

- will + *Verb*
- celebrate
- raise
- have a party (have-had-had)
- festival
- from around the world (*cf.* from)
- each
- share
- about
- country
- way
- build (build-built-built)
- peace

"How can we build peace?" asked Sarah.

"It's just a festival."

"We'll get to know each other.

That's a good start to getting along."

"But I know everyone in our class," said Mary.

"Are you sure?" asked Mr. Pena.

"Did you know that Jama is from Kenya?"

Mary shook her head.

"I don't even know where Kenya is."

"It's in Africa," said Jama.

"That's far away," said Mr. Pena.

"It's another continent."

KEY WORDS

- how
- can + *Verb*
- ask
- just
- get to know (know-knew-known)
- each other
- start
- get along
- everyone

- sure
- Kenya
- shake one's head (shake-shook-shaken)
- even
- Africa
- far away
- another
- continent

"My parents moved here from Russia," said Peter.

"I'm from the Philippines," said Reyna.

"See?" said Mr. Pena.

"We are getting to know each other.

We have three students from different countries!"

KEY WORDS

- parents
- move
- here
- Russia
- the Philippines

- see (see-saw-seen)
- different
- Mexico
- point at
- That's right.

- make (make-made-made)
- do (do-did-done)
- look
- nervous

"And you're from Mexico," said Anne.

She pointed at Mr. Pena.

"That's right," said Mr. Pena.

"That makes four countries."

"What will we do for the festival?"

Reyna looked nervous.

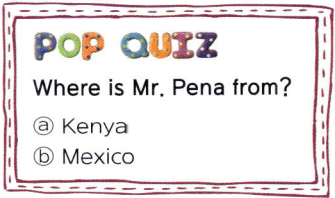

POP QUIZ

Where is Mr. Pena from?

ⓐ Kenya
ⓑ Mexico

"We'll bring our foods," said Mr. Pena.

"I love food!" said Mark.

He rubbed his stomach.

"Yum!"

The boys and girls laughed.

Mr. Pena smiled, too.

"We'll get a taste of lots of things.

Like music, games, and customs."

"It sounds like fun," said Peter.

"We'll visit all the classes," said Mr. Pena.

"We'll see many more countries."

Mary found Mr. Pena's globe.

"We could go around the world," said Mary.

"And never leave our school!"

"Yes," said Reyna.

"All in a single day!"

"That's right!" Mr. Pena spun the globe.

"Bring your families, too. Aha!

It'll be fun for everyone!"

KEY WORDS

- **bring** (bring-brought-brought)
- love
- rub
- stomach
- yum
- laugh
- smile
- too
- **get a taste of** (*cf.* taste)
- lots of
- thing
- like
- game
- custom
- sound like
- fun
- visit
- many more
- **find** (find-found-found)
- globe
- could
- **go around the world** (go-went-gone)
- never
- **leave** (leave-left-left)
- **single day** (*cf.* single)
- **spin** (spin-spun-spun)
- family

A Connect each character with his or her country correctly.

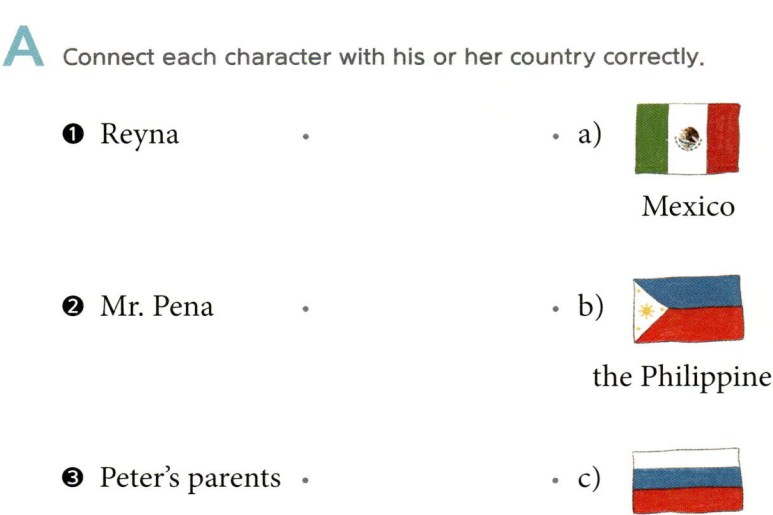

❶ Reyna　　　・

❷ Mr. Pena　　・

❸ Peter's parents　・

・ a) Mexico

・ b) the Philippines

・ c) Russia

B Mark T for true or F for false.

❶ Mary didn't know where Kenya was.　　　　　　T F

❷ Each class would share customs of different countries at the festival.　　　　　　T F

❸ Only two countries would be represented in Mr. Pena's class.　　　　　　T F

❹ The students could bring their families in the festival.　　　　　　T F

C Choose the best answer to each question.

❶ What day is September 21st?

a) the International Day of Fun

b) the International Day of Peace

c) the Day of the Festivals

d) a school holiday

❷ What did students plan to do on September 21st?

a) sharing games and making candies

b) sharing foods and exercising

c) listening to music and drawing pictures

d) learning about customs, foods, and music of each country

❸ What did students and Mr. Pena think about the festival?

a) They thought it would be fun.

b) They knew it would be too hard to plan.

c) They didn't want to have the festival.

d) They weren't at all excited.

Getting to Know Russia

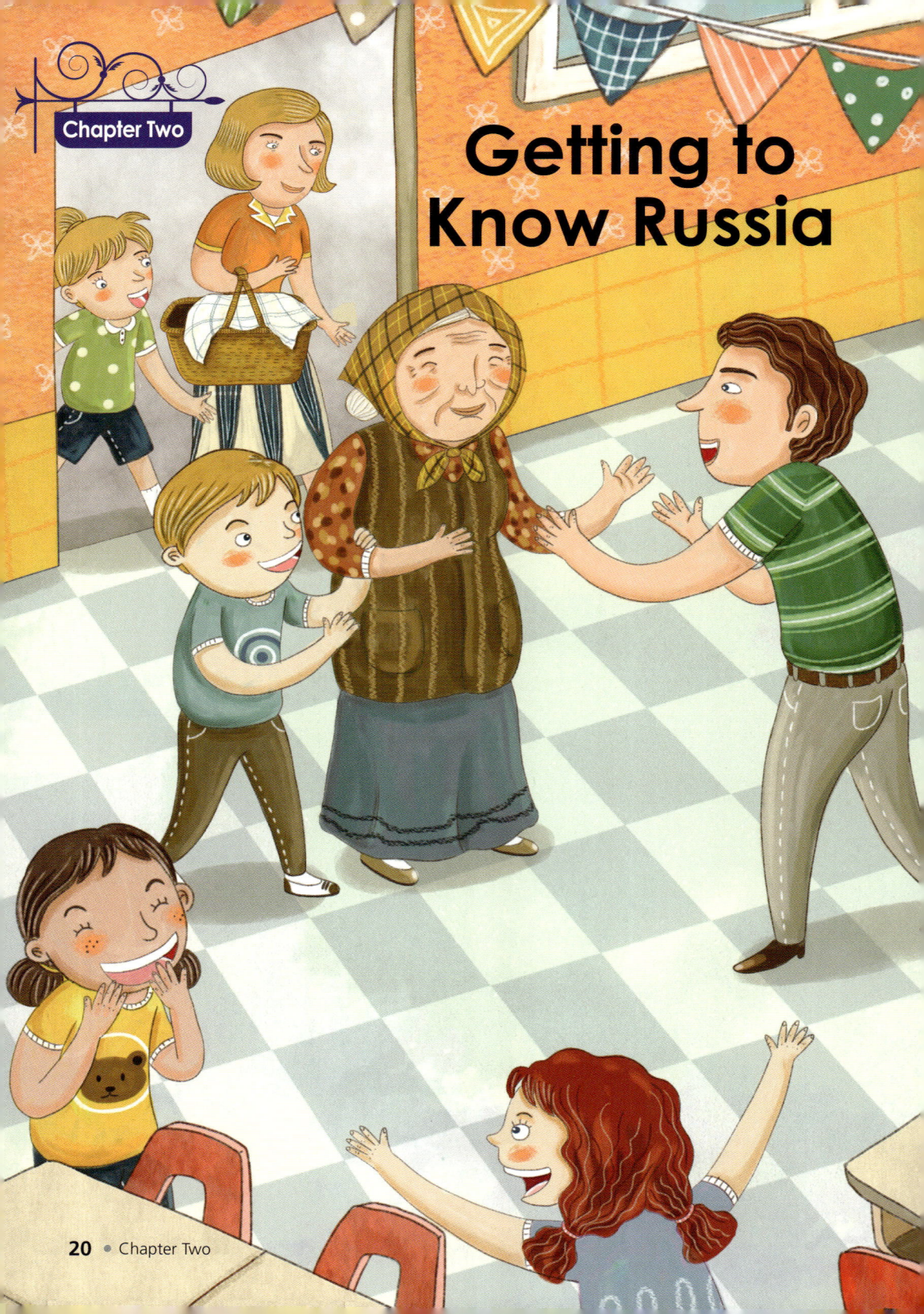

It was September 21st at last!

The families arrived early.

They wanted to help with the festival.

An older woman followed Peter into class.

"This is my grandmother," he said. 🟥Aha!

"It's nice to meet you," said Mr. Pena.

"My babushka lives with us.

She speaks mostly Russian," said Peter.

Peter's mother and sister came next.

They carried a picnic basket.

KEY WORDS

- at last
- arrive
- early
- help with (cf. help)
- older
- woman
- follow
- into
- grandmother

- It's nice to meet you. (meet-met-met)
- babushka
- live with
- speak (speak-spoke-spoken)
- mostly
- Russian
- next
- carry
- picnic basket (cf. picnic / basket)

"We've brought a famous Russian soup," said Peter.

Mark looked in the basket.

"It's very red!"

"It's borscht," said Peter's sister.

"It's made of beets and vegetables."

"I'll try it," said Mark.

He pointed to another dish.

"Are those pancakes?"

"They're Russian pancakes," said Peter's mother.

"They're called blini.

I have berries, too.

You roll up the filling inside."

"Oh, boy," said Mark.

"I'm going to like Russian food!"

▲ borscht

▲ blini

KEY WORDS

- famous
- borscht
- be made of
- beet
- vegetable
- try

- dish
- pancake
- be called (*cf.* call)
- blini
- berry
- roll up

- filling
- inside
- Oh, boy!
- be going to + *Verb*

Peter's sister had something special.

"This is a matryoshka doll."

Sarah joined them.

"It's beautiful," she said.

"And it has a secret," said Peter.

"A secret?"

Sarah picked up the doll.

"It's wooden.

It's heavy, too."

"Give it a twist," said Peter.

Sarah twisted the doll.

"Oh!"

The doll opened!

There was another doll inside.

"It looks almost the same."

KEY WORDS

- something
- special
- matryoshka doll (*cf.* doll)
- join
- secret

- pick up
- wooden
- heavy (↔ light)
- give (give-gave-given)
- twist

- open (↔ close)
- almost
- same

▲ matryoshka dolls

"Try it again," said Peter.

Sarah opened that doll, too.

There was another doll inside!

Sarah opened all the dolls.

She had seven dolls.

They all looked almost the same.

Peter smiled.

"It's a Russian nesting doll." Aha!

He fit all the dolls back together.

"We've been making them since 1890."

Mr. Pena lined up tables in the hallway.

"Let's get ready," he said.

"Here is a table for Russia."

They placed everything on the table.

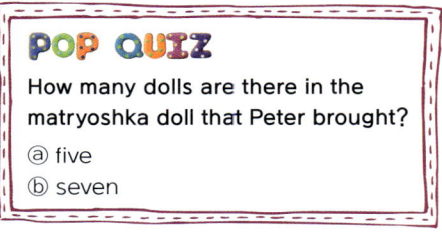

POP QUIZ

How many dolls are there in the matryoshka doll that Peter brought?

ⓐ five
ⓑ seven

KEY WORDS

- again
- nesting doll (*cf.* nest)
- fit back (fit-fit-fit)
- together

- since
- line up
- hallway
- let's + *Verb*

- get ready
- here is
- place
- everything

Then, Peter's mother added a picture.

"It's your wedding," said Peter.

"Russia has a funny custom, right?"

She nodded.

"On our wedding day, the bride's parents steal the bride.

The groom must pay to get her back.

Of course, it's just for fun."

"Just like our festival," said Peter.

"I've learned a lot about Russia!" said Sarah.

"It's so interesting."

"And now we know each other better," said Mr. Pena.

POP QUIZ

What is one interesting wedding custom in Russia?

ⓐ The bride must eat blini.
ⓑ The bride's parents steal the bride.

KEY WORDS

- then
- add
- picture
- wedding
- funny
- nod
- bride

- steal (steal-stole-stolen)
- groom
- must + *Verb*
- pay (pay-paid-paid)
- get back
- of course
- for fun

- just like
- learn
- so
- interesting
- better

 Chapter Two

Comprehension Quiz

A Complete the sentence by connecting each character with the correct explanation.

❶

Peter

a) thought he is going to like Russian food.

❷

Mark

b) had learned a lot about Russia.

❸

Sarah

c) fit all the matryoshka back together.

 B Mark T for true or F for false.

❶ Peter's Russian doll was light. 　　　　　　　T F

❷ Peter's Russian doll was made of wood. 　　　T F

❸ A key was needed to open the Russian doll. 　T F

❹ Peter's Russian doll was seven dolls in one. 　T F

C Choose the best answer to each question.

❶ Peter's "babushka" came to the classroom with him. What does "babushka" mean?

a) Peter's brother

b) Peter's sister

c) Peter's grandmother

d) Peter's dog

❷ What are Russian pancakes called?

a) blini

b) babushka cakes

c) borscht

d) crepes

❸ Who steal(s) the bride for fun in a Russian wedding?

a) the bride's parents

b) the bride's friends

c) the bride's husband

d) the bride's grandparents

Chapter Three

Getting to Know the Philippines

"Where should we go?" asked Reyna.

Reyna pulled a wheeled case.

Her mother carried a box.

"The Philippines!" said Mr. Pena.

"Here is your table."

Reyna's mother put a bowl there.

"I hope I have enough stew."

KEY WORDS

- should + *Verb*
- pull
- wheeled (*cf.* wheel)
- case
- put (put-put-put)
- bowl
- hope

- enough
- stew
- Filipino
- rice
- meal
- pancit
- noodle

- come from (come-came-come)
- China
- Spain
- India
- show up (*cf.* show)

She put another bowl there.

"Filipinos have rice at every meal," she said.

"I have pancit, too."

"Is that noodles?" asked Mark.

Reyna nodded.

"Our foods come from many countries.

China, Spain, even India show up!"

"Here's the dessert."

Reyna's mother added a fourth bowl.

"That's mango," said Mark.

"Is that coconut milk on it?"

"Yes," said Reyna.

"We lead the world in coconuts.

But we wanted to bring halo-halo.

It's a treat for us."

"The ice would melt," said her mother.

"We will bring it another day.

What did you bring, Reyna?"

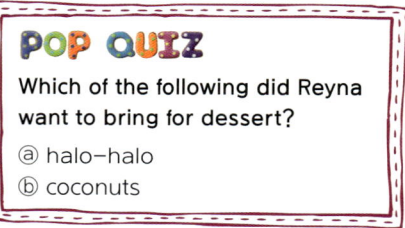

POP QUIZ

Which of the following did Reyna
want to bring for dessert?

ⓐ halo-halo
ⓑ coconuts

KEY WORDS

- dessert
- fourth
- mango
- coconut milk (*cf.* coconut)

- lead the world (lead-led-led)
- halo-halo
- treat
- ice

- would
- melt
- another day

Reyna opened her case.

She placed a yo-yo on the table.

"The word yo-yo came from us.

It's a Tagalog word. Aha!

It means 'come back.'"

Peter picked up the yo-yo and

spun it.

▲ yo-yo

"See?

It comes back.

Plus, now I know Tagalog.

Whatever that is."

Reyna smiled.

"Tagalog is a native language."

"Part of the Filipino language," said Reyna's mother.

"But only half of us speak it.

Many of us speak English."

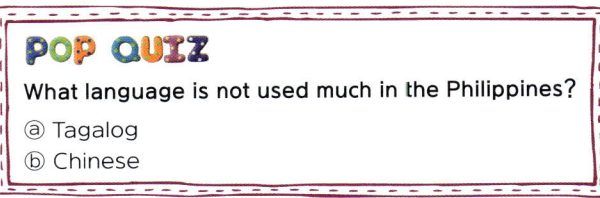

POP QUIZ

What language is not used much in the Philippines?

ⓐ Tagalog
ⓑ Chinese

KEY WORDS

- yo-yo
- Tagalog
- mean (mean-meant-meant)
- come back
- plus

- whatever
- native language (cf. native / language)
- part of
- only
- half

Reyna hung a banner.

The colored flags swayed.

"These are our fiesta decorations."

"Every town has a fiesta."

Reyna's mother held a mask.

KEY WORDS

- hang (hang-hung-hung)
- banner
- colored (cf. color)
- flag
- sway

- fiesta
- decoration
- town
- hold (hold-held-held)
- mask

- honor
- patron saint
- Spanish

"We honor our patron saints."

"Isn't fiesta a Spanish word?" asked Mary.

"Yes," said Reyna.

"It's a festival.

We have many Spanish customs."

▲ the festival that honors the patron saint, the Virgin Mary Peñafrancia
(By Sir Mervs (pinoy biyahero) [CC BY 2.0 (http://creativecommons.org/licenses/by/2.0)],
via Wikimedia Commons)

▲ the Masskara festival, a mask festival, that is held every October in Bacolod City
(By John Albert Pagunsan (http://wikitravel.org/shared/File:Masskara_3.JPG) [CC BY-SA 3.0
(http://creativecommons.org/licenses/by-sa/3.0)], via Wikimedia Commons)

Reyna draped a costume on the table.

"My aunt wore this for a parade."

The dress was red, purple, orange, and green.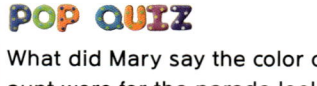

"It looks like a rainbow," said Mary.

"Not everyone will wear costumes.

But there is always dancing at a fiesta.

And feasting and fun," said her mother.

POP QUIZ

What did Mary say the color of the dress that Reyna's aunt wore for the parade looked like?

ⓐ rainbow
ⓑ colored-flag

KEY WORDS

- drape
- costume
- aunt
- **wear** (wear-wore-worn)

- parade
- dress
- look like
- rainbow

- always
- **feasting** (*cf.* feast)

A Which of the following foods is NOT found on the Filipino table at the festival?

a) pancit   b) rice

c) halo-halo   d) stew

B Fill in each blank with the right word(s) below.

come back	patron saints	rice	English

❶ Tagalog and _____ are spoken in the Philippines.

❷ Filipinos have _____ at every meal.

❸ Yo-yo is a Tagalog word that means "_____."

❹ Filipinos honor _____ in the fiesta.

C Choose the best answer to each question.

❶ Who explained where the Filipino table is?

a) Reyna and her father

b) Reyna and her mother

c) Sarah and her mother

d) Reyna's grandparents

❷ What does "fiesta" originally a Spanish word, mean?

a) dance

b) festival

c) parade

d) street

D Mark T for true or F for false.

❶ The Philippines have many Spanish customs. T F

❷ Every town in the Philippines has a fiesta. T F

❸ Filipino foods come from only Spain. T F

❹ Halo-halo is made of rice. T F

Chapter Four

Getting to Know Mexico

"Here is my wife," said Mr. Pena.

"Welcome, Mexico!"

The students cheered.

Mrs. Pena smiled.

"Are all these countries here?"

Mrs. Pena had spied a map.

It was on a wall in the hallway.

"Yes," said Mr. Pena.

"There is Mexico.

We are in North America."

KEY WORDS

- wife
- welcome
- cheer

- spy
- map
- wall

- **North America** (*cf.* north)

POP QUIZ

What continent is Mexico in?
ⓐ North America
ⓑ Asia

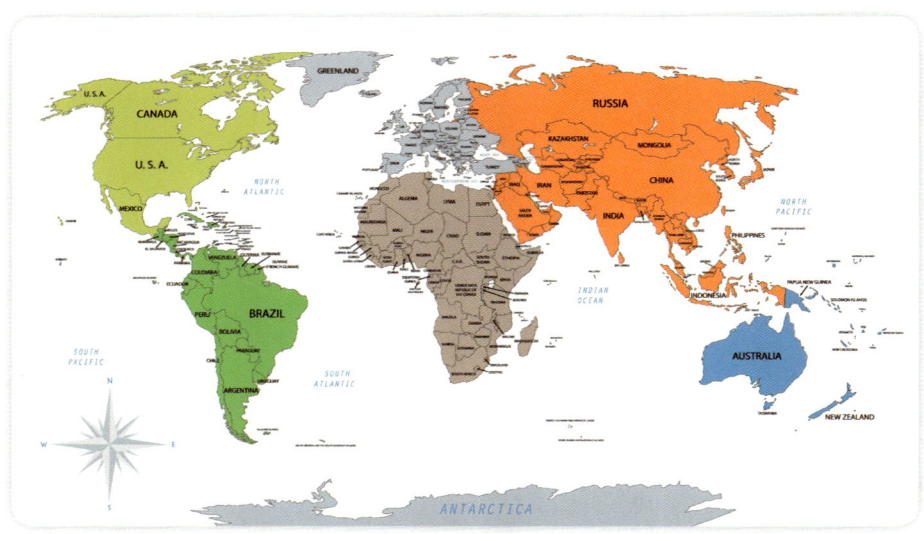

▲ six continents: Asia, Europe, North America, South America, Africa, Oceania

"Look, the Philippines," said Reyna.

"We're in Asia."

"Russia is in Asia, and Europe, too," said Peter.

"Great," said Mark.

"Now I know where the countries are.

But where is the food?

I smell something good!"

KEY WORDS

▪ Asia   ▪ Europe   ▪ great   ▪ smell

Mrs. Pena laughed.

"That's the tacos."

She pointed to a basket.

"We have taco stands on nearly every corner."

Mr. Pena helped unload. **Aha!**

There was pork and chicken.

There were two salsa sauces, too.

He placed the tortillas on the table.

▲ taco

▲ tortilla

KEY WORDS

- taco
- nearly
- corner

- unload (↔ load)
- pork
- chicken

- salsa sauce
- tortilla

"Did you remember the skulls?"

"Skulls!" Mary gasped.

"Are we going to eat skulls?"

Mrs. Pena laughed again.

"No, no," she said.

"These are sugar skulls.

You could eat them, but I wouldn't.

This candy is for the dead." **Aha!**

"Now I'm more confused," said Mary.

KEY WORDS

- remember
- skull
- gasp
- eat (eat-ate-eaten)
- sugar
- candy

- the dead
- confused
- Day of the Dead
- important
- Mexican
- holiday

- be filled with (*cf.* fill)
- be decorated with (*cf.* decorate)
- sequin
- gift
- play

"The sugar skulls are for the Day of the Dead.
It's an important Mexican holiday," said Mrs.
Pena.
She put a basket on the table.
It was filled with small, white skulls.
They were decorated with colored sequins.
"We give our dead gifts and food.
And we play music for them."

"Is Dad coming?" asked Mr. Pena.

"I think I hear him now," said Mrs. Pena.

Music filled the hallway.

"Buenos dias!"

A man playing a guitar joined the class.

"This is my father," said Mr. Pena.

"He is in a mariachi band.

Mariachi is the folk music of Mexico!"

Mr. Pena's father strummed the guitar.

He was dressed in a black suit.

He wore a fancy hat.

"Shall I sing for you?"

"Yes, yes!"

The students gathered around.

KEY WORDS

- **think** (think-thought-thought)
- **hear** (hear-heard-heard)
- **buenos dias**
- **guitar**
- **mariachi**

- **band**
- **folk**
- **strum**
- **be dressed**
- **suit**

- **fancy**
- **Shall I ~?**
- **sing** (sing-sang-sung)
- **gather around**

50 • Chapter Four

A What has nothing to do with the traditional Mexican food called a taco?

a) pork

b) salsa sauce

c) tortilla

d) sugar skull

B Mark T for true or F for false.

❶ Mary was afraid because she thought she would eat real skulls.　　T　F

❷ The sugar skulls were Mr. Pena's favorite dessert.　　T　F

❸ The sugar skulls were for a Mexican holiday.　　T　F

❹ Sugar skulls were decorated with colored sequins.　　T　F

C Choose the best answer to each question.

❶ What is NOT right about the Day of the Dead in Mexico?

a) Mexicans bring gifts for the dead.

b) The day is celebrated with food.

c) The holiday is not very important.

d) There is music for the dead.

❷ What kind of music does a mariachi band play?

a) jazz music

b) the folk music of Mexico

c) classical music

d) country music

❸ What musical instrument did Mr. Pena's father play?

a) piano

b) violin

c) drum

d) guitar

Chapter Five

Getting to Know Kenya

▲ the national flag of Kenya

"Wait for me!" shouted Jama. Her mother and sisters trailed behind her.

"Ah, Kenya," said Mr. Pena. **Aha!** He pointed to Africa on the map.

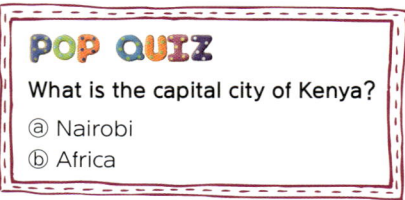

POP QUIZ

What is the capital city of Kenya?

ⓐ Nairobi
ⓑ Africa

KEY WORDS

- wait for
- shout
- trail behind
- more than

- wildlife
- tourist
- safari
- Nairobi

- capital city
- people

"So that's where it is," said Mary.

"You live with elephants and lions!"

Jama's mother smiled.

"Kenya is more than wildlife."

"Tourists love the safaris," said Jama.

"But we are from Nairobi."

"It's the capital city," said her mother.

"Lots of people, no lions."

Jama placed photos on the table.

"We have over 40 different groups in Kenya.

Have you heard of our tribes?" Aha!

"I have," said Peter.

"Isn't that the Maasai?"

He pointed to a picture.

It was a group of women.

▲ a Maasai woman wearing accessories
(By Andreaambia (Own work) [CC BY-SA
4.0 (http://creativecommons.org/licenses/
by-sa/4.0)], via Wikimedia Commons)

"Yes," said Jama.

"See the beads?

They are known for their jewelry.

The Maasai men are famous warriors."

Jama's sisters giggled.

POP QUIZ

What are Maasai women famous for?

ⓐ jewelry
ⓑ warriors

KEY WORDS

- photo
- over
- **group** (*cf*, a group of)
- Have you heard of ~?
- tribe

- Maasai
- women
- bead
- be known for
- jewelry

- men
- warrior
- giggle

"Nyamaza," said Jama's mother.

"That's not English," said Mary.

"Is it Maasai?"

The girls giggled again.

"I said quiet, girls," said Jama's mother.

"The tribes have their own language," she added.

"But many Kenyans speak Swahili."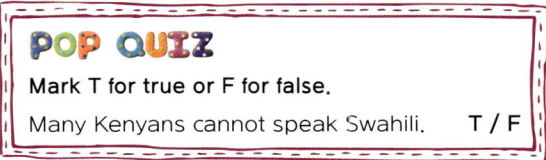

"Like my mother," said Jama.

"It's the national language."

"But you speak English, too," said Peter.

"Most of us speak English," said Jama.

"It helps us understand each other."

POP QUIZ

Mark T for true or F for false.

Many Kenyans cannot speak Swahili.　　T / F

KEY WORDS

- nyamaza
- quiet
- own
- Kenyan

- Swahili
- national language (*cf.* national)
- most of
- understand (understand-understood-understood)

"Many people have come to Kenya.

We are a diverse country." added Jama.

"I don't know that word.

What does 'diverse' mean?" asked Reyna.

"It means lots of variety," said Mr. Pena.

"Our students are diverse."

"Yes, we are very different," said Reyna.

"But we are alike in many ways, too," said Mr. Pena.

"We all like festivals," said Reyna.

"And pretty dresses," said Mary. Aha!

"Games and music," said Peter.

"And food!" said Mark.

POP QUIZ

What does "diverse" mean?

ⓐ lots of variety
ⓑ lots of food

KEY WORDS

▪ diverse
▪ variety

▪ alike
▪ in a way

▪ pretty

Getting to Know Kenya ● **61**

"You must try Kenyan chapati," said Jama's mother.

"Dip it into these vegetables."

"Mmm," said Mark.

"It looks delicious!"

"That's right.

And who would like tea?" asked Jama's mother.

"Chapati and tea go well together."

She poured from a large urn.

"I have brought *chai* for everyone!"

▲ chapati

▲ tea that people enjoy drinking in Kenya

"I thought you said tea," said Mark.

"What is *chai*?"

Jama smiled.

"It's tea," she said.

"It has milk and sugar in it.
Try it!"

Mark took a sip.

"It's delicious!"

"I know," said Jama.

"Kenyans love *chai*.
Adults and children!
We drink it all day
long."

Jama grabbed a drum.

"Now, let's play.

Kenyans love music, too.

And they love their drums!"

She began to pound a beat.

Mr. Pena's father joined her.

He played his guitar.

The hallway rang with a lively tune.

"Look," said Mr. Pena.

He pointed to the map.

"We truly have an international class.

There are four continents here!"

KEY WORDS

- grab
- drum
- begin (begin-began-begun)

- pound
- beat (beat-beat-beaten)
- ring (ring-rang-rung)

- lively
- tune
- truly

64 • Chapter Five

 A Which of the following are related to Kenya? Choose all of them.

a) safari

b) mariachi

c) The Nairobi

d) Tagalog

 B Mark T for true or F for false.

❶ The Maasai is a tribe in Kenya.

❷ The Maasai women are known for their hair.

❸ The Maasai men are famous warriors.

❹ Peter haven't heard of the Maasai tribe.

C Choose the best answer to each question.

❶ What does "Nyamaza" in Swahili mean?

    a) "Come here."

    b) "Let's eat."

    c) "What time is it?"

    d) "Be quiet."

❷ What is NOT right about Kenya?

    a) Nairobi is the capital city of Kenya.

    b) There are over 40 different tribes in Kenya.

    c) Kenyan adults and children love chai.

    d) Kenyans don't love music.

❸ What is chai that Kenyans enjoy drinking?

    a) tea with milk and sugar

    b) coffee with milk

    c) water with sugar

    d) coffee with sugar

Chapter Six

A Surprise Guest

"There are five continents," said a voice.

Everyone turned to see who it was.

Mark grinned.

"This is my Uncle Jack," he said.

"He just returned from New

Zealand!" **Aha!**

Mr. Pena shook his hand.

"I'm glad you could join us!

How long were you there?"

KEY WORDS

- surprise guest
- voice
- turn
- grin

- uncle
- return from
- New Zealand
- shake one's hand

- glad
- how long

"An entire year," he said.

"I was on a working holiday.

It's very common there.

I met lots of young adults.

They come from all over the world.

I'm sorry, though.

I didn't bring food for your festival."

"That's okay," said Mark.

"We're just glad you're back."

▲ the national flag of New Zealand

KEY WORDS

- entire
- working holiday
- common
- all over the world
- sorry
- though
- That's okay.
- be back

"Where is New Zealand?" asked Mary.

Uncle Jack walked to the map.

First, he found Asia.

Then he traced a finger down and right.

"There is Australia," he said.

"So New Zealand is…"

He moved right again…

"There!"

"Is it part of the continent of Australia?" asked Peter.

"It's part of Oceania," said Uncle Jack.

"That includes Australia, too."

"What did you do there?" asked Sarah.

"I worked on farms, mostly," said Uncle Jack.

"It was hard to get used to the seasons," he said. Aha!

"It was hot in December and cold in July!"

KEY WORDS

- walk to
- trace
- Australia
- Oceania
- include

- work on
- farm
- hard
- get used to
- season

- hot
- December
- cold
- July

"Tell them about the Maori," said Mark.

His uncle nodded.

"The Maori are the original natives.

They're the 'people of the land.'

Wait!

I have a postcard."

It was a picture of a man's face.

It had a black swirl design on it.

His tongue was sticking out.

"That's a little scary," said Anne.

"They are not as scary today," said Uncle Jack.

"But you should see the haka."

"The what?" Peter asked.

Uncle Jack snapped his fingers.

"I can show you.

The All Blacks are famous for it.

I made a video," he said.

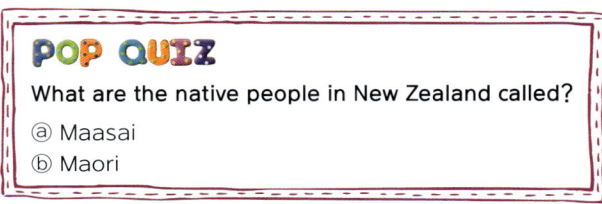

POP QUIZ

What are the native people in New Zealand called?

ⓐ Maasai
ⓑ Maori

KEY WORDS

- **tell** (tell-told-told)
- **Maori**
- **original native** (*cf.* original / native)
- land
- postcard
- swirl
- design
- tongue

- **stick out** (stick-stuck-stuck)
- a little
- scary
- haka
- snap one's fingers
- All Blacks
- make a video

"We'll use your computer, Mr. Pena.
Then the whole class can see."
Mr. Pena started the
video.
"Oh!" said Peter.
"The All Blacks are a
rugby team!" **Aha!**

▲ rugby

"Turn up the volume," said Uncle Jack.

The players crouched and stomped.

They stuck out their tongues.

They beat on their chests.

They yelled and grunted.

▲ All Blacks performing the haka before a game
(By Sonya & Jason Hills from London, UK [CC BY-SA 2.5
(http://creativecommons.org/licenses/by-sa/2.5)], via Wikimedia Commons)

POP QUIZ

What kind of sports team is the All Blacks?

ⓐ baseball team
ⓑ rugby team

KEY WORDS

- use
- whole
- rugby team (*cf.* team)
- turn up

- volume
- player
- crouch
- stomp

- chest
- yell
- grunt

"I can't believe it," said Reyna.

"The haka is a dance."

"Yes," said Uncle Jack.

"It was once a war cry.

Or a way to mark an event."

"Now teams dance before games?" asked Sarah.

Uncle Jack nodded again.

"Many New Zealand teams do.

It's a way to scare their opponents!"

POP QUIZ

Why do ruby teams in New Zealand perform the haka before games?

ⓐ to show their black swirl design
ⓑ to scare their opponents

KEY WORDS

- can't (↔ can)
- believe
- dance
- once

- war cry
- mark
- event
- before

- scare
- opponent

"I have a question," said Mark.

"Are we ever going to eat?"

Everyone laughed.

"I agree," said Mrs. Pena.

"Everything smells so good!" `Aha!`

Mr. Pena called the class together.

"It's time to eat.

There's nothing like a meal to bring people together."

"I'm all for that," said Mark.

"Happy International Day of Peace!"

KEY WORDS

- question
- ever
- agree

- It is time to + *Verb*
- nothing
- bring ~ together

- be all for

A What has nothing to do with New Zealand?

a) Oceania

b) All Blacks

c) Haka

d) Swahili

B Mark T for true or F for false.

❶ A working holiday is unusual in New Zealand. T F

❷ Jack brought New Zealand food for the festival. T F

❸ Jack worked on farms on a working holiday in New Zealand. T F

❹ New Zealand is part of the continent of Australia. T F

Choose the best answer to each question.

❶ Who was the surprise guest that visited Mark?

a) Mr. Pena's father

b) Jama's uncle

c) Mary's brother

d) Mark's uncle

❷ Which one is right about the weather in New Zealand?

a) always sunny

b) cold in July

c) mild all year long

d) windy and wet in December

❸ How long did Uncle Jack stay in New Zealand?

a) half a year

b) a whole year

c) six months

d) three years

Fill in the blanks to review the story.

Title: Around the [W_____] in a Single Day

Setting: September 21st is International Day of [P_____].

Russia
- Borscht is made of [b_____] and vegetables.
- Russian pancakes are called blini.
- Matryoshka is a Russian nesting [_____].

The Philippines
- Their foods come from many countries like China, [S_____], even India.
- [T_____] is a native language.
- Every town in the Philippines has a fiesta.

Mexico
- Mrs. Pena brought tacos.
- The sugar skulls are for the Day of the [D_____].
- Mariachi is the folk [_____] of Mexico.

Kenya
- Maasai is one of the famous [t_____] in Kenya.
- Many Kenyans speak Swahili and [_____].
- Kenyan chapati and tea go well together.

New Zealand
- New Zealand is part of Oceania.
- The Maori are the original [n_____].
- The haka dance was once a [w_____] cry.

Let's Think & Talk

Think about the following questions and answer them freely.

❶ On International Day of Peace, students in Mr. Pena's class got to learn about Russia, the Philippines, Mexico, Kenya and New Zealand in detail. Which country do you think is the most interesting?

❷ If you participated in International Day of Peace festival, which part of your country would you want to tell your friends about?

❸ Besides the countries in the book, do you have any country that you want to know more about? Search for the country and tell your friends about it.

Let's Review the Story

Title: Around the World in a Single Day

Setting: September 21st is International Day of Peace.

Russia
- Borscht is made of beets and vegetables.
- Russian pancakes are called blini.
- Matryoshka is a Russian nesting doll.

The Philippines
- Their foods come from many countries like China, Spain, even India.
- Tagalog is a native language.
- Every town in the Philippines has a fiesta.

Mexico
- Mrs. Pena brought tacos.
- The sugar skulls are for the Day of the Dead.
- Mariachi is the folk music of Mexico.

Kenya
- Maasai is one of the famous tribes in Kenya.
- Many Kenyans speak Swahili and English.
- Kenyan chapati and tea go well together.

New Zealand
- New Zealand is part of Oceania.
- The Maori are the original natives.
- The haka dance was once a war cry.

After-reading **Test**

- Around the World in a Single Day
- Level 1
- 17 Questions

(Vocabulary 5 / Reading Comprehension 10 /

Sentence Structure & Grammar 2)

1. Which of the following word is NOT related to "laughter"?
    ① laugh   ② smile
    ③ yell   ④ giggle

2. Which of the following word does NOT indicate feelings or emotions?
    ① funny   ② nervous
    ③ happy   ④ famous

3. Which of the following is a pair of opposites?
    ① stomp – nod
    ② pound – beat
    ③ common – special
    ④ diverse – different

4. Which pair has the wrong past tense form of the listed verb?
    ① begin – began
    ② lead – led
    ③ think – thought
    ④ wear – worn

5. What is the right word for the blank?

> Peter picked _____ the yo-yo and spun it.

① to   ② off
③ on   ④ up

6. Which of the following countries does NOT correctly match the continent that it belongs?
① Mexico − North America
② New Zealand − Australia
③ Russia − Asia and Europe
④ The Philippines − Asia

7. What is NOT right about the Russian food borscht that Peter introduced?
① It is a famous Russian soup.
② It is a Russian pancake.
③ It is made of beets and vegetables.
④ It is very red.

8. What is the biggest feature of the Russian matryoshka doll that Peter mentioned?
① There are many dolls in one.
② It is made of wood.
③ It has been made since 1890.
④ It is beautiful.

9. What does yo–yo, a toy, whose name originated from Tagalog mean?
   ① travel
   ② sugar skull
   ③ come back
   ④ quiet

10. What is NOT right about the Philippines?
    ① Foods come from many countries.
    ② The Philippines lead the world in coconuts.
    ③ Everyone should wear costumes in a fiesta.
    ④ Many of the Filipino can speak English.

11. What do people prepare for the Day of the Dead in Mexico?
    ① sugar skull
    ② mango
    ③ tacos
    ④ halo–halo

12. How did Mr. Pena explain the meaning of "diverse"?
    ① It means lots of variety.
    ② It means everyone is alike.
    ③ It means we can travel a world in a single day.
    ④ It means there are many countries in the world.

13. What is NOT right about Kenya?
   ① The capital city is Nairobi.
   ② Kenya has over 40 different groups.
   ③ Kenyan chapati and tea go well together.
   ④ Mariachi is the folk music of Kenya.

14. What did Uncle Jack do for one year in New Zealand?
   ① working holiday
   ② festival
   ③ safari
   ④ study

15. What is NOT right about the Maori?
   ① They are original natives in New Zealand.
   ② They have a black swirl design on their faces.
   ③ They perform the haka.
   ④ They speak Swahili.

16. Choose the wrong part of the sentence.

"And pretty dresss," said Mary.
  ①   ②   ③   ④

17. Choose the correct words for the blank.

It was hard _____ to the seasons.

① getting used
② get used
③ that get used
④ to get used

Memo

Memo

Cathy C. Hall

Cathy C. Hall graduated with a broadcasting degree, working in the radio industry as a news reporter and commercial copywriter before going back to school to earn English certification. She spent a decade in education, teaching preschoolers, middle schoolers, and high schoolers. Now, she's a full-time freelance writer, with stories, essays, and poems in publications for both children and adults. Her byline appears in books like *Uncle John's Facts To Annoy Your Teacher*, *Chicken Soup for the Soul's Think Positive for Kids*, *Cup of Comfort for Dog Lovers*, and many more.

 **Smart Readers Wise & Wide 1**-8

Around the World in a Single Day

Written by Cathy C. Hall
Illustrated by Jaehoi Min

First Published in October 2016

Editorial Manager: Juyon Choi
Editors: Jiyeong Park, Kyunghee Jang
Designers: Eunhee Lee, Elim
Cover Designer: Eunhee Lee

Published and distributed by

 Happy House

Darakwon Bldg., 64-1 Jandari-ro, Mapo-gu, Seoul, Korea 04031
Tel: 82-2-736-2031(ext. 250)   Fax: 82-2-732-2037
Homepage: www.ihappyhouse.co.kr
Publisher: Kyudo Chung

ISBN: 978-89-6653-498-2 18740 / 978-89-6653-156-1 18740(set)

[Components]
• 1 Audio CD (Recording Studio: Aram)
• Answer Keys & Korean Translation: Free download at www.ihappyhouse.co.kr